C000183451

PHILIP LARKIN'S
HULL AND EAST YORKSHIRE

by

Jean Hartley

Edited by

Brian Dyson

The University of Hull
Brynmor Jones Library
and
Hutton Press
1995

Published by

The University of Hull
Brynmor Jones Library

and

The Hutton Press Ltd.,
130 Canada Drive, Cherry Burton,
Beverley, East Yorkshire HU17 7SB

Printed and bound by
Clifford Ward & Co. (Bridlington) Ltd.,
55 West Street, Bridlington,
East Yorkshire YO15 3DZ

ISBN 1 872167 74 8

CONTENTS

JEAN HARTLEY

Jean Hartley was born in Hull in 1933. After attending Thoresby High School she worked as a shorthand-typist until she married in 1953. With her husband, George, she founded *Listen* magazine, The Marvell Press and Listen Records. In 1968 they parted and she became a student in the English Department at Hull University. After graduating she worked as a teacher at the Amy Johnson school and then as a lecturer at the Hull College of Further Education. She took early retirement in 1989, the year her autobiography, *Philip Larkin, The Marvell Press and Me*, was first published. She now spends her time writing and painting. She has two daughters.

HOW TO USE THIS GUIDE

This trail has been designed with the walker in mind, including those who have first parked their car or left a bus or train. Nearly all the places mentioned can be reached on foot, although in some cases this might best be after short journeys by car, bus or train. The entries have been arranged geographically, so that it should, with a few exceptions, be possible to walk fairly easily from one location to the next. Maps have been included to show the exact location of each entry.

For the visitor the best starting place is probably Hull, and there is nowhere more logical to start than Paragon Station, which is conveniently also next door to the central bus station.

Once you have explored the entries in central Hull, it is quite easy to reach Cottingham, Beverley and Hessle by bus or train. Lockington, Willerby and Holderness (for places such as Patrington, Withernsea and Skipsea) may also be reached by bus from central Hull.

For those travelling by car there is ample parking in central Hull, Cottingham, and Beverley.

> *Please remember that a number of the entries in this guide are private dwellings, and are therefore not open to the public.*

PHILIP LARKIN: SOME FACTS

1922 Born 9 August in Coventry.

1930 King Henry VIII School, Coventry.

1940 St. John's College, Oxford.

1943 Graduated with 1st Class degree in English. Started work as librarian, Public Library, Wellington, Shropshire.

1945 *The North Ship* published by The Fortune Press.

1946 *Jill* published by The Fortune Press. Assistant Librarian, University College, Leicester.

1947 *A Girl in Winter* published by Faber & Faber. His father died.

1951 Sub-Librarian, Queen's University, Belfast. *XX Poems*, privately printed.

1955 Librarian, University of Hull. *The Less Deceived* published by The Marvell Press, Hessle (run by George and Jean Hartley). Lived at four different addresses in Cottingham.

1956 Moved to flat at 32 Pearson Park.

1958 *The Less Deceived*, read by Larkin, issued on LP by Listen Records.

1964 *The Whitsun Weddings*, published by Faber & Faber. *The Whitsun Weddings*, read by Larkin, issued on LP by Listen Records.

1965 Won Queen's Gold Medal for Poetry.

1970 *All What Jazz* published by Faber & Faber. Visiting Fellow at All Soul's College, Oxford.

1973 Edited *Oxford Book of 20th Century English Verse,* Oxford University Press.

1974 *High Windows* published by Faber & Faber. Moved to house at 105 Newland Park.

1975 Awarded the CBE.

1977 His mother died.

1983 *Required Writing* published by Faber & Faber.

1985 Awarded Companion of Honour. He died on 2 December, aged 63.

PREFACE

In 1955 when Philip Larkin came here, Hull looked, smelled and sounded very different from the way it does now. Natives are inclined to say the town was 'flattened' by the constant pounding it took during the Second World War, and photographs taken at the time show this to be not too wild an exaggeration. By 1955 money was still tight, so little had been done in the way of rebuilding or slum clearance. But there were still enough domes, statues, spires and cranes left to create the romantic skyline Larkin draws for us in his poem *Here*. The high-risers, supermarkets, neat estates, college-complexes and night-spots were to come gradually and later. If you wanted fast food you queued up at the fish and chip shop; for entertainment most people went to the cinema.

Visitors from less industrial places considered Hull to be a distinctively malodorous town. As you moved from one part of it to another your nose would be assailed by tannery, brewery and seed-crushing smells, the reasty stench from the oil and cattlecake mills, and various stinks connected with different aspects of 'the fishing', such as wood-smoking, cod liver oil and fish meal production. Even the politer parts of Hull had their characteristic aromas, pot pourris of open drains and agriculture. One woman remembers the fetid pong of rotting cabbages that came from the fields on Cottingham Road as she walked from the University to her student digs at Thwaite Hall.

The loud sounds in those days emanated not from motors, ghetto blasters and car radios but from the sirens and hooters that signalled to employees in factories and workshops the beginnings and ends of shifts. But although the streets were filled with people, the main noise was the ringing of bicycle bells as workers pedalled off in the morning, at dinnertime and teatime, to and from their homes and queued up six deep at the dozen or so level crossings which cut across the town's roads, until the trains had whooshed past and the gates opened. It is not surprising that Hull used to be known as 'Cycle City'. The more sedate office workers generally travelled on trolley buses, which were frequent and as silent as the trams that had preceded them were noisy.

At night, if you lived in the fishing district, there would be the clatter of clogs as bobbers and filleters went to their work on the fish dock, but all over the town you could hear the baleful call of the fog-horn for, although Hull was cleaner than many industrial towns, most people had coal fires and the factory chimneys belched out endless clouds of smoke. The fogs, in my memory, were thick and ubiquitous.

Hull at that time shared many similarities with Coventry (Larkin's hometown) and Belfast (where he worked before he came to Hull) in its limited scope for leisure activities and the quality of life that could be enjoyed here. There was a general austerity and simplicity that cannot be imagined in the technologically sophisticated but socially distressed 1990s.

During his first year at the Library, Hull University College officially acquired full University status and it and the Library began to grow. Opened in 1928, the University itself is now many times its original size. In 1955 its furthermost building was backed by fields on which seagulls settled and squawked. In that year there were 700 students; three of them, Bob Cryer, Roy Hattersley and Kevin McNamara, were later to become eminent politicians. And since it was nearing the time when many Commonwealth countries would achieve their independence, there was a large intake of overseas students who were here to obtain qualifications before taking up professional posts at home. When Larkin took up his post, with only twelve members of staff, he immediately set to work on plans for Stage I of an urgently needed, purpose-built library.

If my husband and I needed to get in touch with Larkin, for publishing or social reasons, we telephoned him at the Library from a call box a hundred yards away from our house in Hessle, for it was some time before he or we had our own telephone. When he came to see us, he rode up on his large, old-fashioned-looking bike which, sensibly, he sent for from home after taking one look at the flatness of Hull. Our milkman used another form of transport. Each morning he drove up in his pony and trap; his riding boots had the colour and shine of new conkers, and to each of his customers he raised his cap. We lived next door to the 'beer-off'; from its polished wooden counter Alice Turner dispensed brown bottles or pulled pints of draught ale for those who brought their jugs to be filled. We did things differently then.

Many of the more colourful and individual features of Hull

('ships up streets') mentioned in Larkin's poem, *Here*, have disappeared. The cod wars and the general decline in the shipping industry in the 1970s closed the shipyards, the heavy engineering firms that serviced them, and diminished Hull's importance as a shipping port. However, the Slave Museum (Wilberforce House, High Street) is still there and from its back garden you can often see 'barge-crowded water' at high tide as the craft line up to pass through the mouth of the River Hull to the wide estuary of the Humber.

One of the reasons for the popularity of Philip Larkin's verse, is that it is rooted in his everyday experiences and his perceptions of the places around him. During his early years in Hull, Larkin's bike rides down Hessle Road to our house in Hessle, acquainted him with the close-knit streets that housed the fishing community and the 'grim-headscarfed wives'. Passing the town's pet shops with their window displays of cute baby animals would have provoked the feelings of revulsion and sorrow he needed to write *Take One Home for the Kiddies*. Masking the bomb damage were tall wooden hoardings bearing the huge advertising posters that are described in *Essential Beauty*. Those at the junction of Princes Avenue and Spring Bank would be very familiar to Larkin. Many of his poems explore the difference between prosaic reality and the romantic ideal such images represent.

Poems such as *Ambulances*, *Toads Revisited*, *The Whitsun Weddings*, *The Trees*, and *The Building*, show how important this environment was in creating settings for his poetic meditations. If you walk around the streets and roads of Hull and district you can experience for yourself the ambience that affected Larkin in his daily routines and excursions.

Jean Hartley
August, 1995

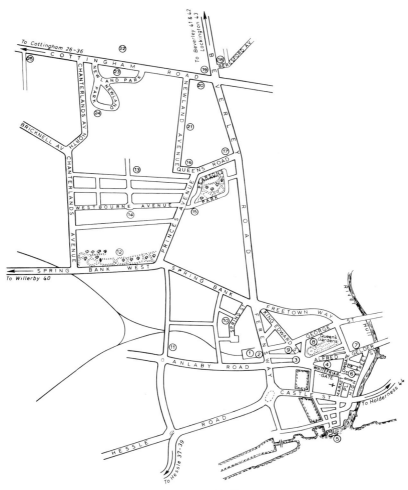

Map 1 : Hull

9

1
CENTRAL HULL

1   HULL PARAGON STATION, Ferensway, *Map 1*

This is a logical starting point, particularly for those arriving by train or by bus (the main bus station is next door). There are also several car parks close by.

Until Larkin learned to drive in 1963, he spent much of his time catching trains. His most life-affirming poem, *The Whitsun Weddings*, encapsulates the journey he took, along with a trainful of newly-weds, from Hull to London. The poem, *Here*, celebrates the memory of a first train journey from the Midlands to Hull and his feelings about the town, its inhabitants and the Plain of

Larkin on board the London train at Paragon Station, c.1964.

Holderness. Travelling by train gives one temporary freedom and irresponsibility. It leaves the mind and the eye open to a host of sensory impressions. That Larkin found it a poetically fruitful way of moving about the country can be seen in poems such as *Dockery and Son* and *I Remember, I Remember*. When the Hartleys recorded Larkin reading *The Whitsun Weddings* volume in 1964, a photograph of the poet peering out of the window of a train on Paragon Station was a natural choice for the record sleeve.

Leaving the station by the main (front) entrance, through the taxi rank and under Paragon House, you will find next door on the right –

2   THE ROYAL HOTEL   *Map 1*

This hotel (formerly the Royal Station Hotel) has been refurbished after a major fire in October 1990 and was re-opened in September 1993. It may best be seen by crossing Ferensway at the nearby pedestrian crossing, and looking back across Paragon Square.

When Larkin had attended some function in the town he would call in here for drinks. There used to be a subterranean restaurant, called The Brigantine, where he would have lunch. Larkin also found the hotel's spacious lounge provided useful neutral territory on which to meet and talk to visitors. His poem, *Friday Night in the Royal Station Hotel*, describes the place in its quieter moments.

Passing by the impressive war memorials to the fallen of the Boer War and the two World Wars, leave Paragon Square via the Barclays Bank corner and walk 400 metres along Paragon Street until you reach Queen Victoria Square. On the left of the Square you will see the multi-domed Town Docks Museum. In front of you, behind the statue of Queen Victoria (with toilets conveniently sited underneath) is the Ferens Art Gallery; whilst, on the right, is –

3   THE CITY HALL, Victoria Square   *Map 1*

Larkin came here to listen to performances by trad jazz bands such as Count Basie, Chris Barber and Acker Bilk.

In the poem, *Broadcast*, he sits in his Pearson Park attic flat listening to a symphony concert being broadcast on the radio from the City Hall, where he envisages the loved one as a member of the audience: 'Your hands, tiny in all that air, applauding'. The University degree ceremonies take place at the City Hall and each year Victoria Square is filled with capped and gowned new graduates

11

being photographed by their parents. In 1973 Larkin gave the citation when his friend, John Betjeman, was awarded an honorary doctorate by Hull University. In the late 1950s and early '60s Sid Gold, a boxing promoter, put on contests at the City Hall which Larkin attended with a friend. He was heard to mutter 'only connect' under his breath during one particularly inept bout. Aware of mounting public concern over the inhumanity of the sport, Larkin seemed bothered that he could not morally defend his enjoyment of it.

Hull City Hall:
degree day procession, 9 July 1982.

Leave the Square by passing across the pedestrian crossing to the right of the Town Docks Museum. Princes Dock and the entrance to Princes Quay shopping centre are on your right. But note the City Wall excavations on display on the left, before passing forward into Whitefriargate (between Burton's on the left and Thornton's on the right), where you will quickly find, on the left-hand side of this busy shopping area –

4   MARKS & SPENCER, Whitefriargate   *Map 1*

Intrigued by the carrier bags toted in after lunchtime expeditions by his (largely) female staff, Larkin paid the shop a visit. The result was his poem *The Large Cool Store*. It should be remembered that M & S was not, in the early 1960s, as relatively upmarket as it has since become.

At this point you have a choice. It is well worth continuing on along Whitefriargate and turning right into Trinity House Lane and along to King Street to visit Holy Trinity Church and the restored Old Grammar School. There are several fascinating streets and alleyways in the area, but the best way to pick up the trail is to leave King Street on the right-hand side via Posterngate to Princes Dock Street.

Alternatively, instead of continuing along Whitefriargate, retrace your steps and turn left into Princes Dock Street, where you will soon reach the junction with Posterngate.

Continue along Princes Dock Street, with the now disused dock on your right (and its shopping centre on stilts), heading towards a large building, Warehouse 6, with a forest of ships' masts behind. There is a pedestrian crossing here (opposite Marina Court) where you can cross the very busy Castle Street. Have a look at the old Spurn Light vessel moored at the Castle Street end of the Marina (which was formerly known as Humber Dock), before walking by the side of the Marina along Humber Dock Street, keeping the vessels on your right. You will soon reach Humber Place, then Henry Vernone Court, and the Humber waterfront. Turn left past the Minerva public house and brewery into Nelson Street (where the magnificent toilets won the 'Loo of the Year' Award in 1990). On your right you will now find –

5   HULL CORPORATION PIER   *Map 1*

Only the ticket office remains to commemorate the ferry. Larkin often used the steamer, as most natives did, not to visit Lincolnshire but just for the ride across to New Holland and back — the only way non-boat-owners could spend time on the river. In the 1964 BBC 'Monitor' film Larkin and John Betjeman can be seen enjoying a windy crossing.

Continue along Nelson Street and, at the statue of Sir William De La Pole (1st Mayor of Hull, 1332), quickly turn left into Queen Street. After 150 metres turn right into Humber Street. Along the way you will pass in front of the 'Manxman' – a club/casino now permanently

Larkin and John Betjeman on the Humber Ferry, 1964.

moored in a former graving dock (note how a section of the bow has been cut out so that it fits over the wall!) – before bearing left to pass by the River Hull Tidal Barrier. Going underneath the unusual Myton Bridge, you will soon reach High Street. Near the junction with Scale Lane is –

6   YE OLDE BLACK BOY, High Street   *Map 1*

This was one of Larkin's favourite pubs in the old part of town. It is close to the river and to Wilberforce House, the 'slave museum'.

Continue along High Street, passing the Hull & East Riding Museum on the right, soon followed, also on the right, by Wilberforce House – the slave museum. At the end of High Street, turn left onto Alfred Gelder Street. Cross the road, with care, and you will soon reach on the right –

7   THE WHITE HART, Alfred Gelder Street   *Map 1*

The Hull Jazz Record Society used to meet here. John White recalls that in 1979 Larkin gave an amusing illustrated talk entitled

'My Life and Death as a Record Reviewer'. Two years earlier, when the Society met at the Black Boy, Larkin talked about Pee Wee Russell and played a selection of his records. Partly because of his deafness, Larkin's preference was always for private rather than public gatherings, no matter how informal, so most often he listened to jazz in his own home or at the houses of John White, John Kenyon or Mike Bowen.

Jazz was one of the great passions of his life and scarcely a day went by without him playing a few records. When he lived in Pearson Park he was under the delusion, fostered by growing deafness, that sound only carried upwards and because he lived aloft in the attic his music would not disturb the other inhabitants.

Continue along Alfred Gelder Street, passing to the right of the statue of Charles Henry Wilson (1833-1907), 1st Baron Nunburn-holme, shipowner and local benefactor, behind which is the Guildhall. Then turn right into Lowgate (City Hotel on the corner), heading towards the monument to William Wilberforce. Cross the road at the pedestrian crossing in front of the monument, and pass into Queen's Gardens. These beautiful gardens, with magnificent floral displays at most times of the year, are built on the site of Hull's first dock, which was filled in in the 1930s. Walk the length of the gardens, emerging almost in front of the Town Docks Museum encountered earlier. Pass right in front of the large circular island containing flowers and fountains. Your way is to the left of the Customs & Excise building on the right, quickly into Vernon Street, right into Savile Street, and right again at the traffic lights into George Street (past the Dram Shop on the corner). A little way along on the right is –

8 BROWN'S BOOKS, George Street *Map 1*

When Larkin came to work in Hull, Brown's were the main local booksellers. At that time he was not a confident man. In fact he asked the Marvell Press (who published his book, *The Less Deceived*, in 1955) to make sure no copies were distributed to Hull bookshops, since he wished to keep his private and his public lives completely separate. However, when the book appeared, to great critical acclaim, he changed his tune and would chase up the Hartleys as soon as Brown's stocks of his book dropped below what he considered to be an acceptable level.

Some readers have confused Larkin with the speaker in his poem, *Fiction and the Reading Public*. Nothing could be more misleading

15

than to associate him with the opinion that 'books are a load of crap'. Books were not only his livelihood but also a lifelong passion and solace. His boyhood excitement at discovering the Coventry Central Library, his extensive personal collection of books and his participation in the setting up of the publishing concern which eventually became Hull University Press, attest his addiction to the printed word.

Return down George Street (left out of the Bookshop), and cross at the traffic lights into Jameson Street. Crossing King Edward Street (this part is pedestrianised) you immediately reach on the left –

9   DYNASTY CHINESE RESTAURANT, Jameson Street (opposite Fletcher's)   *Map 1*

This has changed hands many times over the years but it was Hull's first Chinese restaurant. The Hoi Sun, as it was called then, seemed very exotic in the early 1960s. Larkin often ate here with friends.

Carry on along Jameson Street, crossing Ferensway in front of Paragon Station and pass to the right of the station, through the bus station and left into Short Street (with bus garage on the right). Cut right across St. Stephen's Square, past the snooker club and the Providence Inn, and into Spring Street. One hundred metres along on the left you come to –

10   HULL TRUCK THEATRE, Spring Street   *Map 1*

It used to be called Spring Street Theatre and its beginnings involved much community effort. Larkin did not care for the theatre but he came here whenever there was something on that interested him. One such event was *Pres*, an Alan Plater jazz opera with music by Bernie Cash, about Lester Young and his friendship with Billie Holiday. In 1990 Spring Street staged *Sweet Sorrow*, a play by Alan Plater at which Larkin was posthumously present. The story concerned four oddly-assorted fans who met at the Larkin memorial service in Westminster Abbey. Since then they have organised a party once a year on St. Valentine's night, in his honour, and now, four years later, they have an unexpected guest — the man himself. The actor, John Scarborough, made a creditable and witty ghost.

Return to St. Stephen's Square and turn right into St. Stephen Street, passing Beverley House (headquarters of Northern Foods) to the junction with Park Street. If you turn left into Park Street and onto the bridge over the railway you will gain excellent views of Paragon Station on the left and, on the right, thirteen storeys tall –

11   HULL ROYAL INFIRMARY, Anlaby Road   *Map 1*
'Higher than the handsomest hotel', is the opening line of his poem *The Building*, written in 1972 and published long before he was to become so well-acquainted with it. A year earlier he had written, and published in the magazine *Wave* (Sonus Press), the poem *How* ('How high they build hospitals'), perhaps a practice shot for the longer poem. It is the implicit destination of *Ambulances*.

2
WEST HULL

You now have two main choices. The simplest is to retrace your steps to the bus station and catch one of the regular buses heading for the junction between Spring Bank and Princes Avenue and point 12 on the trail. Alternatively, for really keen walkers, it is quite feasible to continue the trail on foot by continuing along Park Street, turning right at the traffic lights onto Anlaby Road and along 400 metres to the Hull Royal Infirmary. It is then about half a mile to the next location, gained by turning right at the roundabout onto Argyle Street, over the railway bridge until it becomes Derringham Street, and turning left into Spring Bank. If you continue past the second set of traffic lights to the pedestrian crossing over Spring Bank you will reach –

12   SPRING BANK CEMETERY (Botanic/Princes Avenue end)
Map 1

This is the old part of the cemetery. When Larkin came to Hull it was neglected and had become riotously overgrown. Larkin described it to John Betjeman as 'the most beautiful spot in Hull' and to the local council (who had threatened to clean it up beyond recognition) as 'a natural cathedral, an inimitable blended growth of nature and humanity of over a century; something that no other town could create whatever its resources'. When the Hartleys asked him where he would like to be photographed for the sleeve of their LP record of him reading *The Less Deceived*, this was the place he chose.

Leaving the cemetery, we now return to the junction of Spring Bank and Princes Avenue, turning left up Princes Avenue. After about 400 metres, and crossing over six streets or avenues on the left, turn left into Westbourne Avenue. This conservation area is well worth exploring –

13   THE AVENUES   *Map 1*

The four avenues that run off Princes Avenue: Victoria, Park, Westbourne and Marlborough were much loved by Larkin through all the seasons of the year. Being only five minutes away from his

Larkin and John Betjeman in the Spring Bank Cemetery, 1964.

Pearson Park flat made them very handy for town walks and a quick change of scene.

Heading along Westbourne Avenue to the roundabout junction with Salisbury Street (with its magnificent cast iron fountain-cum floral display) you soon reach, on the left –

14   THE HULL NUFFIELD HOSPITAL, Westbourne Avenue
Map 1

During his last illness Philip Larkin stayed here several times. Though he was very ill, visiting friends found him smartly dressed

The Hull Nuffield Hospital (drawing by Jean Hartley).

and as entertaining as ever in a room overlooking the back garden. Comic hypochondria and intimations of mortality had been regular motifs in his conversation from young manhood onwards, so lugubrious warnings such as, 'You'll probably be the last people to see me alive', had less effect on his visitors than they warranted. It was here that he died on 2 December 1985. His last words, to the nurse who held his hand, were 'I am going to the inevitable'.

Retrace your steps along Westbourne Avenue. If you cross Princes Avenue at this point you immediately reach a pedestrian entrance to Pearson Park, where after a short distance on the right you will see –

15 32 PEARSON PARK *Map 1*

The house was once owned by the University. Its three storeys of flats were intended as temporary havens for staff who were new to the town and who were expected to move out to become owner-occupiers of more desirable premises once they had settled in and had time to get to know the area. Philip moved into the attic flat in 1956 and stayed there for the next eighteen years! He said that he

32 Pearson Park (drawing by Jean Hartley).

Larkin and John Betjeman in the former's Pearson Park flat, 1964.

had always lived at the top of buildings and that it pleased him to do so. It was the perfect place for a man of his temperament, one who loved to look out at the world but who wanted complete control over who could look back at him. His green-fringed eyrie provided the ideal ambience for writing and was obviously the starting point for poems such as *Toads Revisted*, *The Trees*, *High Windows*, *Sad Steps*, *Broadcast*, and *Vers de Société*. The poems that comprise *The Whitsun Weddings* and *High Windows* volumes were written here as were many poems that would have been included in a last collection had there been one. They can be found in *The Collected Poems*, edited by Anthony Thwaite (Faber & Faber). Much of the 1964 BBC 'Monitor' programme footage, in which John Betjeman interviewed Larkin, was filmed in this flat. In 1974 the University decided to sell the house and Larkin was obliged to look for somewhere else to live. The house, called 'Carisbrooke', now bears a plaque bearing the name of its famous former resident.

Continue along the park road parallel with Princes Avenue, past the pond on the right until you reach the pedestrian exit on the left just beyond the children's playground, returning you to Princes Avenue. Turn right onto Princes Avenue and right again onto Queen's Road at the roundabout. Next to the roundabout is –

16   THE QUEEN'S, Queen's Road   *Map 1*

and a little further along Queen's Road is –

17   ST. JOHN'S HOTEL, Queen's Road   *Map 1*

Both pubs were a few hundred yards away from Larkin's Pearson Park flat. When he went to the Queen's with a woman friend he would often choose the quiet cocktail bar to the right of the entrance, away from the lounge which was usually full of students. He tended to visit the more homespun St. John's when on his own.

Continue along Queen's Road to the junction with Beverley Road, turning left at the traffic lights. Pass under the railway bridge, cross at the pedestrian crossing, and proceed along Beverley Road (over the traffic lights at the junction with Clough Road and Cottingham Road) until you reach just beyond the Beresford Avenue junction on the right, where you will find –

22

18   578   BEVERLEY   HIGH   ROAD   (corner   of   Beresford Avenue)   *Map 1*

A girl friend of Larkin's used to live here, with her family. Larkin was often invited for Sunday supper and always arrived between five and ten minutes after the appointed time. He later confessed to her that he usually arrived at the door too early and spent twenty minutes or so walking up and down the road. When she asked why, he said he felt it wasn't the done thing to turn up earlier than you were bidden, but to be up to ten minutes late gave the polite amount of grace.

Retracing your steps and crossing over Beverley Road at the pedestrian crossing, you soon reach the junction with Cottingham Road (traffic lights) where you should turn right past –

19   THE HAWORTH ARMS (junction of Beverley Road and Cottingham Road)   *Map 1*

Which is followed quickly on the left (opposite Haworth Street) by –

20   THE   GARDENERS'   ARMS   (Beverley   Road   end   of Cottingham Road)   *Map 1*

After leaving work, Larkin would often stop off at one of these pubs for a quick drink before going home.

Carry on along Cottingham Road, where you will soon reach a junction with traffic lights. The road on the left, with a large domed Methodist Chapel on the corner, is –

21   NEWLAND AVENUE   *Map 1*

The variety of its shops makes it a very popular shopping area. It is usually crowded and therefore easier to negotiate on foot. Larkin regularly bought his food here. Later, when he bought a car, he complained about its hazards for drivers.

After passing over Auckland Avenue, Cranbrook Avenue and Ferens Avenue you will reach, on your right –

22 THE UNIVERSITY OF HULL, Cottingham Road   *Map 1*

Plans of the campus can be obtained from the Reception Office in the large Administration Building immediately on your left.

Larkin and Ted Hughes in the Middleton Hall,
May 1975.

22a   The Middleton Hall

This was built in the 1960s. It is the University's main arts centre and is used for plays, special lectures, musical recitals and jazz concerts. Its subterranean gallery houses a fine permanent collection of paintings and sculptures and mounts regular visiting exhibitions and lecture series. Larkin came to many of the Hall's functions and occasionally introduced visiting lecturers, such as Ted Hughes. After Larkin died Donald Roy of the Drama Department presented to the general public a Philip Larkin thanksgiving evening on 30 June 1986, when his friends and colleagues reminisced about the Philip Larkin *they* knew.

Before the Middleton Hall was built all public lectures, meetings, dances and theatricals took place in the old Assembly Hall which was in what used to be known as the Science Building and is now called the Cohen Building. It is here that the long unfinished fragment *The Dance* (*Collected Poems*, p.154) is set.

The Brynmor Jones Library, external view.

Larkin and his Library staff, 1957.

Larkin and his senior staff (including his 'loaf-haired' secretary) during the making of the BBC 'Monitor' film, 1964.

22b The Brynmor Jones Library

In an interview in *The Observer* in December 1979 Larkin said: 'Librarianship suits me... and it has just the right blend of academic interest and administration that seems to suit my particular talents, such as they are'. The Brynmor Jones Library will be of prime interest to the visitor since it was Larkin's place of work for over thirty years and largely his creation. He modestly described its history in his pamphlet, *A Lifted Study-Storehouse: the Brynmor Jones Library 1929-1979* (re-issued by Hull University Press in 1987). The Library's archives hold a large collection of Larkin's

Andrew Motion, Douglas Dunn and Philip Larkin
outside the Brynmor Jones Library, November 1979.

letters, manuscripts and workbooks, along with first editions of all his books. It also includes articles, translations, critiques, biographies and audio and video tapes. Scholars may apply to the University Archivist for permission to consult available material contained in the archive.

Only staff and students of the University may enter the Library, although it is possible for non-members to gain access to it if a prior appointment has been made.

22c Staff House

This is now used as a social centre for staff and students. It is open to members of the public. It contains a bar, restaurants, a cafeteria, coffee drinking areas and offers a choice of formal and informal meals. Larkin spent most of his lunchtimes here talking and drinking with friends and colleagues. His group was not noted for its quietness and restraint.

Leave the campus the way you entered, go over Cottingham Road at the pedestrian crossing, and turn right, passing in front of –

High office windows? Larkin in his Library office, 1981.

23   OLD GREY MARE HOTEL (opposite the University)   *Map 1*

Until recently this was the Newland Park Hotel, offering a wide range of food. Here Larkin entertained the various architects and builders who came to work on the Brynmor Jones Library. Over the years the University has invited many distinguished poets such as Robert Lowell, William Empson, D. J. Enright, Ted Hughes,

Blake Morrison, Andrew Motion, and John Wain, to come and recite their work. After the readings Larkin would be part of the group which repaired to the hotel, with the guest of honour, for refreshment and conversation.

Continue along Cottingham Road and turn left into Newland Park. Keep right at the junction, and then cross over to reach (on the right-hand side of the road) –

24   105 NEWLAND PARK   *Map 1*

'I have bought the ugliest one-roomed house in Hull', was how, with typical exaggeration, he described to a friend his 1974 Newland Park purchase. The responsibilities of home ownership weighed heavily upon him. Not least was the problem of how to keep the garden in trim. Always tender hearted over animals, his anguish at having accidentally killed a hedgehog while mowing the lawn, can be seen in his poem, *The Mower* (*Collected Poems*, p.214). He lived in this house from 1974 until his death in 1985.

105 Newland Park.

29

Retrace your steps to Cottingham Road, and turn left, crossing at the traffic lights over Chanterlands Avenue. After about 400 metres you will reach –

25   THE GOOD FELLOWSHIP, Cottingham Road   *Map 1*

This is a mock-Tudor pub situated conveniently close to the University. Larkin came here often during his early years in Hull. He said its dimly lit ambience reminded him of London pubs.

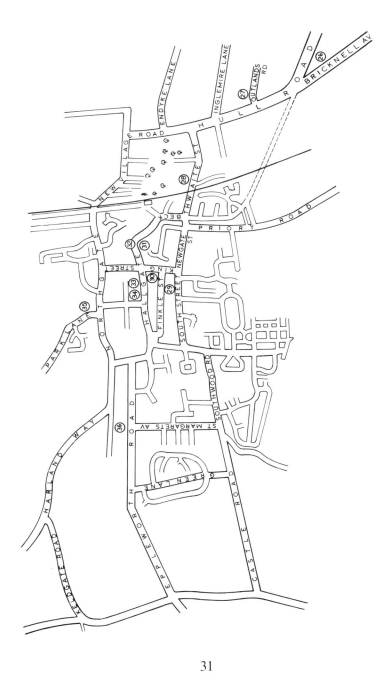

Map 2 : Cottingham

3
COTTINGHAM

Again, it is feasible to continue the trail by walking along Cottingham Road and then Hull Road until you reach point 26 (see below) on the left. Alternatively, you can travel by car, by bus from the University, or by bus or train from Hull, to the next main centre, Cottingham.

The main bus and car routes pass by first, at the junction of Cottingham Road and Bricknell Avenue –

26   THE WEST BULLS   *Map 2*

This newish pub, close to the University, was a popular lunch place for Larkin whenever he wanted a quiet chat with a friend or colleague.

Then, on the right-hand side as you continue along Hull Road towards Cottingham, after about 400 metres –

27   11 OUTLANDS ROAD, Cottingham   *Map 2*

These were Larkin's second digs in which he stayed from April to June, 1955. The landlady was kindly but her radio was so noisy that it prevented him from writing. (He told the Hartleys he would like to build a public convenience for camels over the grave of Signor Marconi). Nevertheless, and significantly, he managed to finish writing *Mr. Bleaney* (begun in Belfast) soon after arriving in Hull.

Continue along Hull Road towards Cottingham, turning left at the roundabout into Thwaite Street. This road contains several large University of Hull student halls and houses, including, on the right-hand side close to the railway level crossing and opposite Crofter's Drive –

28   HOLTBY HOUSE, Thwaite Street, Cottingham   *Map 2*

The one-time home of Winifred Holtby's family is now a University-owned students' hall of residence. This was Larkin's first billet following his arrival from Belfast in March 1955. He told a friend that he felt as if he were lying in some penurious doss-house with hobos snoring and quarrelling all around him.

29 THE MEMORIAL CLUB, Elm Tree House, South Street, Cottingham *Map 2*

This may be viewed from either South Street or Finkle Street (towards the King Street end).

In 1976, Larkin, and a group of men from all walks of life, regularly met in the Men's Bar at the Duke of Cumberland. When the landlord, anticipating the Sex Discrimination Act, relaxed the rules, the male sanctum was invaded by snooker-playing young men and their girl friends. The older regulars, Larkin included, felt the character of the place had changed and took refuge at the private (members only) Memorial Club where women were welcome only at lunchtimes, weekends and on Thursday evenings. Larkin took his women friends to lunch there but mostly he appeared on his own. Members remember him coming in about three evenings a week and sitting quietly in a corner with his drink and detective novel. Over the evening he would consume three pints of bitter and two scotches. He took an interest in everyone who talked to him and was particularly animated if the conversation turned to cricket. Although he didn't play snooker, he watched others play and clearly found the Club's atmosphere very relaxing and congenial. One member, a bookmaker called Malcolm Stroud, recalls that during a lengthy ceremony, robed and waiting to be invested as Mayor of Beverley, he asked Larkin: 'What would you give for a pint?' The answer is reported to have been:

> I would be willing
> To go to ten shilling.

30 DUKE OF CUMBERLAND, King Street, Cottingham *Map 2*

Located alongside the Market Square, on King Street.

This pub sold famous sandwiches: good crusty bread with delicious filllings. Larkin often ate lunch and drank here.

31 ST. MARY'S CHURCH, Hallgate, Cottingham *Map 2*

The funeral was held here on 9 December 1985. A large congregation composed of friends, acquaintances and colleagues gathered to remember Philip Larkin and to sing some hymns he liked:

Larkin's funeral, St. Mary's Church, Cottingham, 1985.
Left-right: Charles Monteith, Kingsley Amis, Hilary Amis, Kitty Hewett.

'Abide with me'; 'Lead kindly light', and 'The day thou gavest, Lord, is ended'. The service was conducted by Rev. Terence Grigg. Kingsley Amis spoke movingly and amusingly about his late friend. The cortège was followed by Larkin's sister Kitty, his niece Rosemary, Kingsley Amis and his ex-wife Hilary Kilmarnock, Andrew Motion and Charles Monteith.

32   HALLGATE, Cottingham   *Map 2*

In later years, friends and acquaintances often bumped into Larkin when they were buying their groceries. Once, while waiting in the delicatessen, Janet Duffin (his ex-neighbour), complained to him that she found queueing an awful waste of time. Larkin replied that, on the contary, he regarded queueing as a welcome respite in a succession of meaningless activities.

33   192a HALLGATE, Cottingham   *Map 2*

This private house is located next to Wilburn Court on the left-hand side of the road as you face the centre of Cottingham.

Larkin moved into the top flat of this property in June 1955. Mr. and Mrs. Drinkwater, the owners, had a very noisy young daughter. Larkin doubted if he would ever, aside from the grave, find the silence he so longed for, and which was crucial for his writing. Nevertheless, he was fond of their rabbits and, even after he moved out, he offered to come and take care of the animals when the Drinkwaters went on holiday.

34   200 HALLGATE, Cottingham   *Map 2*

This was located on the site of what is now Wilburn Court, with the surviving 192 Hallgate now next door.

This was Larkin's third abode in Cottingham, although he stayed here for only a week or two in June 1955. His landlady, Mrs. Squire, was 'a nice old thing' who played her radio quietly but the place itself was too small and not comfortable enough for him.

35   KING GEORGE V PLAYING FIELDS, Northgate, Cottingham   *Map 2*

The entrance to these playing fields is immediately opposite the Northwood Club on Northgate.

This was the inspiration for *Afternoons*, one of Larkin's most moving short lyrics on the eroding effects of time. He watches the young mothers pushing their children on swings and observes that at the same time 'Something is pushing them/To the side of their own lives'.

36   MUNICIPAL CEMETERY, Cottingham, Plot no. 81   *Map 2*

The entrance to the cemetery is immediately opposite the junction of St. Margaret's Avenue and Eppleworth Road, and there is a telephone box on the corner. Larkin's grave is located on the left-hand side as you enter, in the sixth row in from the trees on the far side. The white headstone simply says 'Philip Larkin 1922-1985, Writer'. A few graves away in the next (seventh row) is the grave of Sir Brynmor Jones and his wife Dora, who died four and two years respectively after Larkin.

It is fitting that Philip Larkin's remains should rest in the locality in which he chose to live for the greater part of his adult life. The everyday sights he encountered inspired many of his poems and

Larkin's grave, Municipal Cemetery, Cottingham.

much of his best work was written here. As he wrote in his foreword to *A Rumoured City* (Bloodaxe Books, 1982), a collection of poems by local poets: 'A place cannot produce poems: it can only not prevent them, and Hull is good at that'.

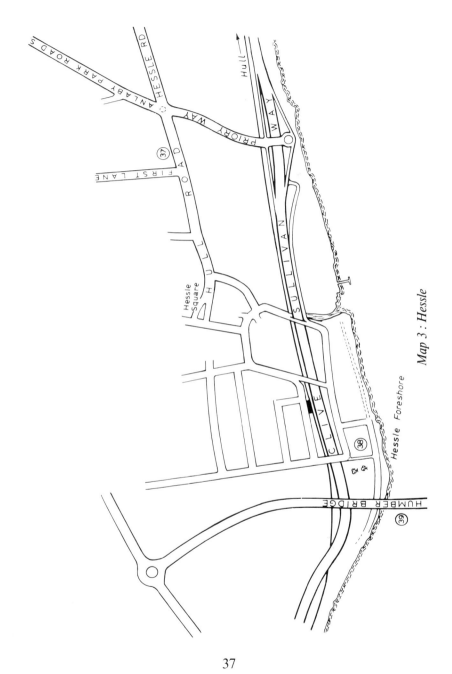

Map 3 : Hessle

4
HESSLE/WILLERBY

Hessle may easily be reached by car. Also, there are regular bus services to and from Hull and Beverley, together with a railway station.

37   253 HULL ROAD, Hessle   *Map 3*

This small terraced house can be found next door to a toy model shop about half a mile from the centre of Hessle heading towards Hull, near the junction of Hull Road and First Lane.

This was the home of George and Jean Hartley, founders of *Listen* magazine, The Marvell Press and *Listen* records.

After including Larkin's poems in the early issues of *Listen*, the Hartleys wrote to him in Belfast asking him if he had enough poems to form a collection to inaugurate their new imprint, the Marvell Press. He sent them what became *The Less Deceived* and, at about the same time, accepted the post of Librarian at the University of Hull. The book, published in 1955, established Larkin's reputation as a poet and the Hartleys' as publishers. Aside from their professional association, Larkin became a friend and regular visitor until 1970 when the Hartleys divorced and George moved to London. The friendship with Jean continued and is documented in her autobiography, *Philip Larkin, The Marvell Press and Me* (Sumach Press). Subsequent tenants have altered the Victorian bay window and the front door of their former home.

38   HESSLE FORESHORE   *Map 3*

The foreshore and Humber Bridge viewing areas are well signposted in the area. There is ample car parking, and the railway station is not far from the foreshore.

When Larkin visited George and Jean Hartley, they would sometimes take a walk, with the Hartley children, to Hessle Haven and along the foreshore. It is a good place from which to comprehend the isolated nature of Hull and to view the far bank of the river Humber, 'where sky and Lincolnshire and water meet' (*The Whitsun Weddings*).

39   THE HUMBER BRIDGE, Hessle   *Map 3*

This is rather difficult to miss!

'A swallow fall and rise of one plain line' — Larkin felt ambivalent about the building of it, not least because the authorities deemed that the bridge's existence rendered the Hull ferry obsolete. However, Larkin agreed to write the libretto for a 'Bridge for the Living', set to music by Anthony Hedges.

Anthony Hedges and Philip Larkin, composer and librettist, 'Bridge for the Living, 1981.

40   THE GRANGE PARK HOTEL, Willerby   *Map 4*

This hotel may clearly be seen from the new A164 Beverley-Humber Bridge Road (on the right heading towards Beverley), just beyond the Willerby roundabout and shopping complex.

39

In 1968 Larkin invited C. Day Lewis to be the first Compton Poetry Fellow. Endowed by Joseph Compton, a literature-loving philanthropist, the Fellowship required the incumbent to visit the University fortnightly in term, to lecture once a term and to meet students informally in the Poetry Room of the Library next day for a poetry seminar. It was an added distinction for Hull that, after accepting the Fellowship, Day Lewis was made Poet Laureate. In 1969 Larkin gave a farewell dinner for Day Lewis at the Grange Park Hotel, to which he invited twelve people.

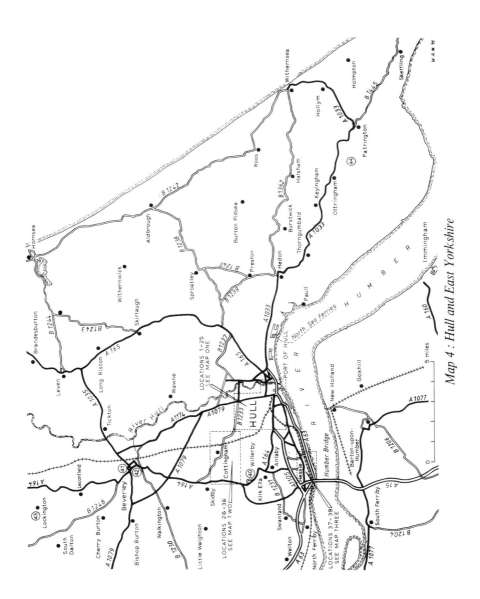

Map 4 : Hull and East Yorkshire

41

5
BEVERLEY

41   BEVERLEY TOWN   *Map 4*

There are good public transport links between Hull and Beverley (bus or train), and Hessle and Beverley (bus), and ample parking space in the centre of the town.

Larkin liked making shopping expeditions to Beverley which had a good range of choice food shops, but as he grew older he transferred his shopping allegiance to Cottingham which was just down the road from his home in Newland Park.

42   BEVERLEY ARMS, North Bar Within, Beverley,   *Map 4*

This is located almost opposite Beverley's second most notable landmark, St. Mary's Church. This Church, along with the dominating Beverley Minster, can clearly be seen on approaching the town, and the two together represent a good way of finding your bearings.

During Larkin's early years in Hull, he spent most weekends cycling, either on his own or with a friend, round the East Riding and getting to know the area. 'It is very nice and flat for cycling' (letter to Ansell and Judy Egerton). On the way back he invariably stopped for tea at the Beverley Arms.

6
LOCKINGTON

43   LOCKINGTON HOUSE COTTAGE, Church Lane, Lockington   *Map 4*

Realistically, the small but attractive village of Lockington is reachable only by car – but is well worth the visit if you can make it. It was home for many years of the Remington (typewriter) family. Church Lane is dog-legged in shape. The cottage is on the left of the church as you go into the church car park, beside the big house from which it takes its name.

When Malcolm Bradbury came to work at Hull University, he and his wife, Elizabeth, bought a cottage in this attractive village. After they had moved on they rented the cottage to Richard Murphy when he came to the University for the year as Compton Poetry Fellow. Larkin often visited the Bradburys, and Murphy whom he had known from his Belfast days.

7
HOLDERNESS

44 THE PLAIN OF HOLDERNESS *Map 4*

A tour of Larkin country would be incomplete without visiting Holderness. This is simple by car – head out of Hull to the east on the A1033 aiming for Hedon, Patrington, Kilnsea, Withernsea or Sunk Island. However, there are also good bus services to the larger towns and villages, such as Patrington and Withernsea.

This area lies between the Wolds and the coast and it extends from a little south of Bridlington to Spurn Point. Philip Larkin loved the area, its remoteness, its romantic-sounding names — Cherry Cob Sands, Stone Creek, Skeffling, Sunk Island — and the long lanes where you could get quite lost. You could go back there to look for a particular place or road, especially in summer when the hedgerows were so lush, and never again be able to find it. The first half of 'Bridge for the Living' brilliantly evokes this region where 'wide, wind-muscled wheatfields wash round villages/ Their churches half-submerged in leaf'.

In his autobiography, Hubert Nicholson describes the villages of Holderness as 'marshy places with grass like wire and millions of insects and white and red flowers and the sweet brier that smelled like hot apple pie' (*Half my Days and Nights*, p.24). At the eastern edge of this thinly populated plain lies the sea; each year it batters the cliffs and bears away large tracts of land. Larkin felt the poignancy of this 'seasonal decrease'.

Other writers have shared Larkin's affection for Holderness. Edward C. Booth (1872-1954) was a particular favourite of Larkin's. Booth, a gifted cellist and composer, settled in Scalby, near Scarborough, and wrote eight novels set in this area (Aldbrough, Skeffling, Withernwick, etc.). A modest man, his work was much admired in its day and some critics compared him to Thomas Hardy. Larkin enjoyed the humour and realism of his writing and, of course, shared his feeling for the 'unfenced existence' depicted in his books.

Larkin's preface to *A Rumoured City*, is the finest tribute the area could wish for. It is instinct with his gratitude at having found a place that was the perfect metaphor for his own sense of belonging and separateness:

> People are slow to leave it, quick to return. And there are others who come, as they think, for a year or two, and stay a lifetime, sensing they have found a city that is in the world, yet sufficiently on the edge of it to have a different resonance. Behind Hull is the plain of Holderness, lonelier and lonelier, and after that the birds and lights of Spurn Head, and then the sea. One can go ten years without seeing these things, yet they are always there, giving Hull the air of having its face half-turned towards the distance and silence, and what lies beyond them.

ACKNOWLEDGEMENTS

The photographs have been supplied by the University of Hull Photographic Service. The maps have been drawn by Wendy Munday from drafts by Laurien Waldie and Stephen Wright. The two drawings are by Jean Hartley. For all the help they have given me in compiling this booklet, I should like to thank Phil Bacon, Maeve Brennan, Jill Carter, Brian Dyson, Daphne Glazer, Alison Hartley, Chris Ketchell, Frank McNaughton, Ted Tarling, and John White.

FURTHER READING

Larkin, Philip, *Collected Poems* / edited by Anthony Thwaite (Marvell/Faber, 1988).

Larkin, Philip, *Selected Letters* / edited by Anthony Thwaite (Faber, 1992).

Larkin, Philip, *Required Writing: miscellaneous pieces, 1955-1982* (Faber, 1983).

Larkin, Philip, *'A Lifted Study-Storehouse': the Brynmor Jones Library 1929-1979* (Hull University Press, 1987).

Bamford, T. W., *The University of Hull: the first fifty years* (Oxford University Press, 1978).

Dunn, Douglas, ed., *A Rumoured City: new poets from Hull* (Bloodaxe Books, 1982).

Dyson, Brian, ed., *The Modern Academic Library: essays in memory of Philip Larkin* (Library Association, 1989).

Hartley, George, ed., *Philip Larkin 1922-1985: a tribute* (Marvell Press, 1988).

Hartley, Jean, *Philip Larkin, the Marvell Press and Me* (The Sumach Press, 1993).

Holtby, Winifred, *South Riding* (Collins, 1936).

Motion, Andrew, *Philip Larkin: a writer's life* (Faber, 1993).

Nicholson, Hubert, *Half my Days and Nights* (Autolycus, 1982).

Pevsner, Nikolaus, and Neave, David, *Yorkshire: York and the East Riding* (The Buildings of England series) (Penguin, 1995).

Spooner, Derek, 'Places I'll remember — Larkin's "Here"', *Geography*, no. 335, v.77(2), 1992, pp.134-142.

PHILIP LARKIN MEMORIAL SERIES
No. 3

General Editor: Brian Dyson,
Archivist, University of Hull

This pamphlet series is intended to honour the memory of one of the University of Hull's longest-serving and most famous officers, Philip Larkin. Apart from works of a biographical nature, its scope is limited to those aspects of librarianship, bibliography and literature with which Philip Larkin and/or the Brynmor Jones Library are particularly associated.

Already published:

No.1: *'A Lifted-Study-Storehouse': the Brynmor Jones Library 1929-1979*, by Philip Larkin, updated to 1985, with an appreciation of Philip Larkin as Librarian, by Maeve Brennan.

No.2: *The Labour archive at the University of Hull*, by John Saville.

Prospective contributors to the series should contact:

> Brian Dyson,
> University Archivist,
> Brynmor Jones Library,
> University of Hull,
> Hull,
> England,
> HU6 7RX.